DOUBLE MATRIX FINANCIAL SAVINGS SYSTEM

Lanakila Washington

creating wealth in a very simple way!

forward

I honor the God within for downloading this information to me to share and to help others in saving money and creating a nice nest egg of wealth for now and the future.

I pray that this book will be the door opened for all to walk through and enjoy the blessings of prosperity. So be it.

Welcome to Your Financial Blessings!

Greetings! My name is Lanakila Washington. I created this system after long days and nights over time, contemplating how I could make money, save money, and help others do it as well. I read several books and watched videos on line, listening to how others made and saved money.

Then I thought about what I created when I ran for Public office back in 2008. It was called the SRS plan. The Supplement Retirement Savings Plan was a project that I worked on. It was to be introduced to Congress as a law to be passed for the wealth and security of all Americans. I recently learned that many people retired or on disability have a cap on how much money they can keep in the bank. Moreover, retirement plans offered by banks are not available due to the Federal Government placing that cap on their money.

After writing the President about the issue and getting a direct response, I determined to create a reality where all Americans/anyone in this world with a desire to save money could do it in a simple way. Thus, the Double Matrix Financial Savings System plan was created. There are several amounts charted that you can choose and follow through based on how much you can afford to start with and how much you want to have in your account at the end of six months and or one year.

View the charts and make your choice. As long as you follow the system, you will end up with the amount stated in your account. All of the savings are based on a month to month schedule but the amount is not month to month as you will see when you view the chart.

As your money grows and you reach the 5th to 6th or 11th to 12th month and the amount suggested to deposit falls out of your budget, just split that amount into two or three deposits in the month or scretch the year into two to three months more to make the deposits. This may happen to those of you who receive money once a month. You can also get yourself a debit card like the BlueBird American Express card that I have. They have a nice savings feature where you can put money away. Some banks have the same savings feature too if you wish to save with your current bank.

 BE SURE TO TAKE A LOOK AT THE BONUS OFFER AT THE END OF THIS BOOK!

$5.00 Matrix Plan.

MONTH 1 - $5.OO	MONTH 7 - $15.00
MONTH 2 - $15.00	MONTH 8 - $30.00
MONTH 3 - $30.00	MONTH 9 - $60.00
MONTH 4 - $60.00	MONTH 10 - $120.00
MONTH 5 - $120.00	MONTH 11 - $240.00
MONTH 6 - $240.00	MONTH 12 - $260.00
TOTAL SAVED: $470.00	TOTAL SAVED: $725.00 = $1,195.00

Note: if months 5,6, 10, 11, and 12 is over your budget to save, simple make month 5, & 6 $30 and $60 and months 10:$15, month 11:$30 and month 12:$60, you will have a lower result but still effective. This step can be done with any one of the plans where the months apply.

--

<u>$10.00 MATRIX PLAN.</u>

<u>MONTH 1 - $10.00</u>   <u>MONTH 7 - $20.00</u>

<u>MONTH 2 -$20.00</u>   <u>MONTH 8 - $40.00</u>

<u>MONTH 3 - $40.00</u>   <u>MONTH 9 - $80.00</u>

<u>MONTH 4 - $80.00</u>   <u>MONTH 10 - $160.00</u>

<u>MONTH 5 - $100.00</u>   <u>MONTH 11 - $40.00</u>

<u>MONTH 6 - $120.00</u>   <u>MONTH 12 - $80.00</u>

<u>TOTAL SAVED:$370.00</u>   <u>TOTAL SAVED:$420.00= $790.00</u>

<u>$20.00 MATRIX SAVINGS PLAN A</u>

<u>MONTH 1 - $20.00</u>   MONTH 7 - $40.00

MONTH 2 - $40.00	MONTH 8 - $60.00
MONTH 3 - $60.00	MONTH 9 - $80.00
MONTH 4 - $80.00	MONTH 10 - $100.00
MONTH 5 - $100.00	MONTH 11 - $120.00
MONTH 6 - $120.00	MONTH 12 - $140.00
TOTAL SAVED:$420.00	TOTAL SAVED:$540.00 = $960.00

PLAN B SAVINGS

MONTH 1 & 2 IS THE SAME AS IN PLAN A

MONTH 3 - $80.00	MONTH 7 - $60.00
MONTH 4 - $160.00	MONTH 8 - $80.00
MONTH 5 - $80.00	MONTH 9 - $160.00
MONTH 6 - $160.00	MONTH 10 - $60.00
	MONTH 11 - $120.00
	MONTH 12 - $240.00
TOTAL SAVINGS:$540.00	TOTAL SAVINGS:$700.00 = $1,240.00

$35.00 MATIX PLAN

MONTH 1 - $35.00   MONTH 7 - $70.00

MONTH 2 - $70.00   MONTH 8 - $90.00

MONTH 3 - $140.00   MONTH 9 - $110.00

MONTH 4 - $110.00   MONTH 10 - $130.00

MONTH 5 - $130.00   MONTH 11 - $150.00

MONTH 6 - $150.00   MONTH 12 - $170.00

TOTAL SAVINGS:$635.00   TOTAL SAVINGS:$720.00 = $1,355.00

Note: You can also do what I call a "rollover" where as after you have completed month 1 - 6, or 7 - 12, you can repeat any one of the 6month cycles. You can be creative and combine your cycles like 6months from this cycle and 6 months from another cycle plan! or run more than one plan, one to a savings account and the other to a debit or credit card. If you are paid on a weekly or by-weekly basis, you can double up by following the plan each time you get paid which will increase the amount and perhaps the time in which you meet the saving goals at the end of the cycle.

$40.00 MATRIX SAVINGS PLAN A.

MONTH 1 - $40.00   MONTH 7 - $80.00

MONTH 2 - $80.00   MONTH 8 - $100.00

MONTH 3 - $100.00   MONTH 9 - $140.00

MONTH 4 - $140.00   MONTH 10 - $160.00

MONTH 5 - $160.00   MONTH 11 - $180.00

MONTH 6 - $180.00   MONTH 12 - $200.00

TOTAL SAVED:$700.00   TOTAL SAVED:$860.00 = $1,560.00

$40.00 PLAN B.

MONTH 1 - $40.00   MONTH 7 - $40.00

MONTH 2 - $80.00   MONTH 8 - $80.00

MONTH 3 - $160.00   MONTH 9 - $40.00

MONTH 4 - $180.00   MONTH 10 - $80.00

MONTH 5 - $80.00   MONTH 11 - $40.00

MONTH 6 - $160.00   MONTH 12 - $80.00

TOTAL SAVED:$700.00   TOTAL SAVED: $200.00 = $900.00

-

$50.00 MATRIX SAVINGS PLAN

MONTH 1 - $50.00   MONTH 7 - $100

MONTH 2 - $100.00   MONTH 8 - $120.00

MONTH 3 - $120.00   MONTH 9 - $140.00

MONTH 4 - $140.00	MONTH 10 - $160.00
MONTH 5 - $160.00	MONTH 11 - $180.00
MONTH 6 - $180.00	MONTH 12 - $200.00
TOTAL SAVED: $750.00	TOTAL SAVED: $900.00 = $1,650.00

-

There you have it. Six fabulous ways to save money, make it grow and enjoy the benefits of it all. I trust that this will change the way you save money and will make you better fit financially.

Lets change the reality of not having enough to always having more than we ever need. Thank you and congratulations!

Lanakila Washington

moneyfitnessnow@yahoo.com

THE BONUS!

I connected to my good friend Robert Hollis and he shared with me that he has come out of Network Marketing retirement because of the awesome opportunity he had at helping his wife give back to animals. I trust Robert and his decision making when it comes to Network Marketing so I took a look at what he got into and I was excited! My other friend that was on board with Robert, Craig Jackman, hit me up on Face Book, I jumped in and I'm glad that I did.

 The products offered are second to none and the financial opportunity has unlimited potential to bring wealth to those who follow the system and do the work. I'am committed to helping others duplicate a system that will be beneficial in every way. So when you visit my sites, you will have the chance to meet Robert!

I want you to check out this fabulous system. wait to you see all the information in this free tour! Make sure you add your name and email before clicking to take the free tour!

http://www.HempWorxBizOp.com/staywellnow/?source=biz

http://www.CashBackTravelBiz.com/staywellnow/?source=travelbiz

I know you will love what you see. It is my blessing to share this information with you. I enjoy seeing folks make and save money and enjoy radient health. Thats my purpose of writing this book and I hope you will take full advantage. Aloha!

Lanakila Washington

-

NOTES:

notes: hows it going for ya?

NOTES ON HOW YOU'RE DOING AFTER 3 MONTHS SAVINGS

DON'T FORGET TO TAKE THE FREE TOUR FROM THE BONUS OPTION!

YOU DESERVE TO BE RICH!

YOU ARE WORTHY!

LIFE IS GOOD AND I'AM PRESENT WITH JOY

I'AM LIVING MY DREAM

LIFE IS BLISSFUL

THE TIME IS NOW TO TAKE ACTION!

I'AM ALWAYS ALINED WITH WELL BEING

<u>I LOVE KNOWING THAT I'AM RADIENTLY HEALTHY</u>

I LOVE KNOWING THAT PROSPERITY IS ALL AROUND ME.

I'AM THANKFUL FOR ALL THAT I HAVE

AND I'AM EAGER FOR MORE.